MOSCOW

"The capital city of Moscow" ("Sigismund's" drawing of Moscow). Compiled by Johann Gottfried Philip Abelin and devoted to King Sigismund III. 1610

MOSCOVIA VRBS METROPOLIS TO:
tius Ruſsiæ Albæ.

Moſqua fluuius

Intima pars vrbis dicta Kitaigorod

Secunda pars vrbis, suo circumdata muro, dicta Bielgorod

Tertia pars vrbis versus Septentrionem vocata Skorodum

MERID. OCCID. ORI. SEPT.

The Moscow Kremlin

The Kremlin, "the heart of the Russian state", is a unique architectural ensemble occupying an area of 28 hectares in the centre of Moscow, and its history is inseparably linked with the history of the capital of Russia.

The first mention of Moscow dates from 4 April 1147, when Yuri Dolgoruky (or "Long-Handed"), the Prince of Suzdal, met here, on the border of his possessions, with Sviatoslav, Prince of Novgorod Seversky. The year 1156 marks the second chronological mention of Moscow in the Chronicles. It reads as follows: "Grand Prince Yuri Volodimerich founded the town of Moscow at the mouth of the Moskva River". This "town", a precursor of the contemporary Kremlin, was an outpost in the possessions of the Vladimir-Suzdal princes on the border with the principalities hostile to them. Moscow was a wooden fortress about two hectares in area built at Borovitsky Hill at the confluence of the Moskva and Neglinnaya Rivers. In several centuries the fortress was three times radically rebuilt and expanded – under Ivan Kalita, Dmitry Donskoy and Ivan III. Today it is the political centre of the Russian Federation, the President's residence, and one of Russia's largest museums.

The military history of the Moscow fortress in the first two centuries was quite dramatic. It was repeatedly besieged and burnt down both by Russian princes, rivals of the Vladimir-Suzdal rulers, and the Mongol khans, who invaded North-Eastern Rus in 1238.

The citadel was named the Kremlin only in the 14th century. The Moscow Chronicle for the year 1331 reads: "...there was a fire in Moscow and the town of Kremlin burnt down." The origin of the word "Kremlin" is traced back to *krem*, that part of the woods where the best timber could be found. It is likely that it has been associated with the construction of new oak fortress walls around the enlarged territory of the Kremlin in the reign of Ivan Kalita in the 1340s. They began to include an ancient square east of the original citadel – the present-day Sobornaya (Assembly) Square. Along the perimeter of this square the prince built Moscow's first stone churches.

The fires of 1354 and 1365 inflicted a great damage to the Kremlin fortifications and after them Dmitry Donskoy, the Grand Prince in 1359–89, built the earliest stone Kremlin of white limestone in 1367–68. The territory of the Kremlin was then enlarged again and it became similar to its present-day outlines.

In a century the white-stone walls became so dilapidated that the Italian Ambrogio Contarini, who visited Moscow in 1476–77, thought that they were wooden. Indeed, holes and gaps in the walls were patched up by wood. Therefore in 1485 Ivan III, the Grand Prince in 1462–1505, began to construct the now surviving Kremlin walls and towers in red brick. At the same time Ivan Kalita's churches in the Kremlin were rebuilt and the construction of new stone palaces and chambers for the sovereign was started. This work was carried out between 1485 and 1516 by the efforts of the Italian architects who came to Moscow following the court of Ivan III's second wife, Sophia Paleolog, who had been educated at the papal court in Rome. Sigismund von Herberstein, who made his first visit to Moscow in 1514 and the second in 1526, was delighted: "The fortress is so large that besides the Sovereign's chambers, fairly large and well built in stone, it has the Metropolitan's wooden chambers as well as those of the Grand Prince's brothers and very many other persons. Besides, there are many churches in the fortress so that it is reminiscent of a town."

Under the first Tsars of the new Romanov dynasty the Kremlin had a major reconstruction: the complex of the royal apartments was refurbished (1635–36), the new Patriarch's Palace was erected, the churches were painted anew and the Kremlin towers were crowned with tall stone tent-shaped towers.

In 1812 Napoleon Bonaparte's headquarters resided in the Kremlin. Before leaving Moscow the French exploded some Kremlin buildings. It was then that several towers, including the Ivan the Great bell-tower, were destroyed and the churches were ravaged. Reconstruction work was carried out in 1816–19 under the direction of Osip Bove.

The next major reconstruction was undertaken in the late 1830s – early 1850s, during the reign of Nicholas I (1825–55), when the architect Konstantin Thon built the Great Kremlin Palace and the Armoury.

After the revolution of 1917 the Kremlin became the residence of the Soviet government. A large-scale restoration of ancient monuments was carried out. Nevertheless at the same time the Kremlin ensemble suffered great and irreparable losses: the early Chudov (Miracle) and Resurrection Monasteries, the Church of the Saviour-in-the-Woods and other structures were demolished.

The Moscow Kremlin

The Walls and Towers of the Moscow Kremlin

The architect who mainly inspired the creation of the present-day Kremlin fortifications was Aristotle Fioravanti (*c*. 1420 – *c*. 1486), a well-known fortifier and military engineer, who arrived in Moscow in 1475 from Bologna in Northern Italy. The work was done under the guidance of the Milanese architects Pietro Antonio Solari, Aleviz (Aloisio) de Cartisano and Marco Ruffo and the Venetian Antonio Friazin. All of them represented the Italian school and one of its masterpieces is the Sforza Castle in Milan. The Northern Italian architects, however, created in Moscow a much larger structure and taking into consideration the specific features of the terrain, a much more elaborate architectural complex. The overall length of the Kremlin walls is about 2.2 kilometres. Along the upper edge of the walls run walkways protected by 1045 battlements in the form of "swallow's tail" and once covered by a gable roof. The towers were provided with machicolations – floor openings between the supporting corbels of battlements, and special chambers for fighting ground battles. The earliest tower constructed to protect the Kremlin was the Tainitskaya Tower founded in 1485 (architect Antonio Friazin). One of the latest was the barbican Kutafya Tower (1516, architect Aleviz Stary). The towers, originally covered by wooden tent-shaped roofs, in the 17th century acquired their picturesque many-tiered stone tops, which have twice increased their height. This complex of works started in 1625 with the construction of the Saviour Tower by Christopher Galloway and Bazhen Ogurtsov (around 70 metres high) intended for the installation of the famous chimes. In the second half of the 17th century the Spasskaya (Saviour), Nikolskaya (St Nicholas), Troitskaya (Trinity), Borovitskaya (Forest) and Vodovzvodnaya (Water Pump) Towers were crowned with armorial eagles. In the 1930s they were replaced by red stars of ruby glass in gilded frames.

The Saviour
Tower.
The Water Pump
Tower.
View of the walls
and towers
of the Kremlin
from the Kremlin
Embankment
of the Moskva
River

The Moscow Kremlin

The Ivan the Great Bell-Tower

The celebrated structure dominating the entire Kremlin skyline till the early 18th century belongs to the rare type of churches intended "for the bells". In 1329 Ivan Kalita began to construct the first church of this kind in the centre of Assembly Square. The church was built in a single summer season and consecrated on 1 September of the same year in honour of St John Climacus. In 1505–08 the architect Bon Friazin created a much larger building more than 55 metres high. Moreover, in 1600, by orders of Tsar Boris Godunov, it was built over and reached the height of 81 metres. In 1532–43 a massive belfry wall (architect Petrok Maly) appeared near the church. In the centre of its upper tier was designed a large room for the main bell of the Kremlin. In the 18th century plans were conceived to replace it with the Tsar Bell, the world's second in size (weighing about 20 tonnes and 6.2 metres high), cast in the 1730s by the founder Ivan Motorin. But they had no time to lift the bell and during a devastating fire in 1737 the bell cracked and since then has remained near the bell-tower. Not far from the Tsar Bell one can see another superb example of the art of casting resting on a decorative platform – the Tsar Cannon, the world's largest medieval bombard (length 5.34 metres; caliber 890 millimetres). Cast of bronze by Andrey Chokhov in 1586, it belonged to the defensive artillery of the Kremlin.

View of the Ivan the Great Bell-Tower
from Ivanovskaya Square.
The Tsar Bell.
The Tsar Cannon

The Assumption Cathedral

This beautiful five-domed building, which looks monolithic ("as a single stone"), stands at the highest point of Borovitsky Hill and in the course of several centuries was the main church of Russia; it was here that all the Russian Tsars, including Nicholas II (on 14 May 1896), were crowned for the throne.

The cathedral is a successor of Ivan Kalita's Assumption Cathedral, on the site of which in the early 1470s, by orders of Ivan III, began the construction of a new majestic edifice. Originally the work had been done by Moscow craftsmen, but their creation collapsed in the spring of 1474. On 26 March 1875 the Ambassador Semion Tolbukhin brought from Italy Aristotle Fioravanti, who began to implement a grand-scale project enthusiastically. The new church about 45 metres high was erected just in four years. Russian contemporaries duly appreciated Fioravanti's work. The Chronicle reads: "The church was marvellous thanks to its grandeur, height, lightness, resplendence and space…" The cathedral was consecrated on 12 August 1479.

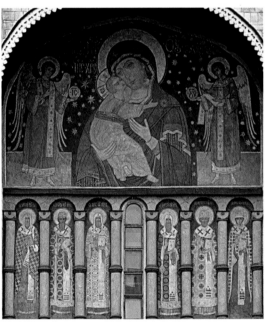

The Assumption Cathedral. View from the south-east
Fresco over the south portal with the image of the Mother of God of Vladimir. Created by craftsmen led by Simon Ushakov. 2nd half of the 17th century.
Interior of the Assumption Cathedral

The Archangel Cathedral

The earliest Church of the Archangel Michael, especially revered by the princes as the Archistrategus, Leader of the Heavenly Host, was built in the Kremlin as early as the 13th century and became the princely burial vault. In the summer of 1333 Ivan Kalita erected in the Kremlin a stone cathedral consecrated on 28 September. The first person buried in it on 1 April 1341 was Ivan Kalita himself. In 1505–09 the architect Aleviz Novy put up the present-day building of the cathedral with tall lancelated *zakomaras*-conches. All the tombs of the 14th and 15th centuries were transferred from Ivan Kalita's church into it. Until the early 18th century the cathedral retained the status of burial vault of the Russian monarchs. In the second half of the 16th century it was decorated with murals by orders of Ivan the Terrible. A special place among the paintings was given to the portraits of all eminent princes of the Vladimir-Suzdal-Moscow branch. In 1652–66 the murals were almost totally repainted, but the earlier subjects and compositions were not altered. In the 1680s the iconostasis was also replaced, but its principal decoration has remained the superb icon of Archangel Michael, a work of the Moscow school of the turn of the 14th and 15th centuries.

Interior of the Archangel Cathedral with a view of the iconostasis.
The Archangel Cathedral. View from the south-east.
Archangel Michael. Moscow school. Late 13th – early 14th century

The Annunciation Cathedral

The Annunciation Cathedral served as the domestic church of the Moscow princes and was a part of the ruler's courtyard complex. It had a predecessor built, most probably, as far back as 1291. It is known that the basements of the cathedral served as a grand ducal treasury. In 1405 the cathedral was painted by Theophanes the Greek, Prochorus from Gorodets and Andrey Rublev; they also produced icons for the iconostasis. On 6 May 1484, according to the Moscow chronicler, Ivan III founded the new chambers in the Tsar's Courtyard and next to them erected the Annunciation Cathedral. The construction was led by architects from Pskov, who created a church with stepped vaults crowned by three domes. The central vault was gilded, therefore the cathedral became known as the "Golden-Topped Cathedral". The cathedral was linked with the princely chambers by galleries. In the centre of the cathedral iconostasis was placed the Deesis by Andrey Rublev. In 1547, during the reign of Ivan the Terrible, a devastating fire destroyed the cathedral and it was restored only in 1563–64. The cathedral, the floors of which are paved with agate-like jasper, were decorated with new murals and icons by Andrey Rublev from the Assumption Cathedral of the Simonov Monastery; in the cathedral's galleries were created chapels crowned with domes. As a result of this work the cathedral became a five-domed church.

The Annunciation
Cathedral. View from
the north-east.
Frescoes in the cathedral
gallery.
Iconostasis
of the Annunciation
Cathedral.
Jasper with agate insets

Church of the Deposition of the Robe and the Terem Churches

A small, architecturally elegant single-domed and four-pillared Church of the Deposition of the Robe was constructed in 1484–85. In the 17th century it was connected by a covered gallery with the Terem Palace and in 1653 became a part of the complex of domestic churches of the Russian tsars and tsarinas. This complex includes, besides the Church of the Deposition of the Robe, five churches: from the western end the Terem Palace adjoins the early Church of the Nativity of the Virgin (1393–94), and in the east, the Verkhnespassky Cathedral (the Cathedral of the Saviour-at-the-Top), standing over the Chamber of Sophia Paleolog, the Church of the Crucifixion of Christ, built over the Verkhnespassky Cathedral, the Church of the Resurrection (or of St Eudocia) next to it and the Church of St Catherine under it. In the 1680s Osip Startsev united the eastern churches of the Terem under a general roof crowned with eleven small gilded decorative cupolas on tall drums.

Iconostasis in the Church of the Deposition of the Robe.
Church of the Deposition of the Robe. View from the east.
Domes of the Terem churches.
Murals in the Tsar's Prayer Room in the Terem Palace.
Iconostasis of the Upper Cathedral of the Saviour

The Faceted Chamber

The Faceted Chamber, a simple yet imposing cubic building faced with rusticated (or faceted) stone slabs, is the most ancient surviving part of the palace ensemble of the Tsar's Courtyard. The ensemble, with its history traced back to the Terem of Yuri Dolgoruky, included the wooden princely chambers, which were partly rebuilt in stone in the reign of Ivan III. The same Tsar also ordered to build the Faceted Chamber, the Tsar's Main Throne Room, which was put up by the Italian architects Marco Ruffo and Pietro Antonio Solari between 1487 and 1491. The building juts out to Assembly Square, from which the Red Porch, a wide staircase for ceremonial processions, leads to its second floor. On the ground floor of the chamber were arranged five rooms for domestic needs; the second floor has two official interiors. These are the huge one-pillar Throne Room (459 square metres, 9 metres high) and the Holy Corridor linking the chamber with the palace complex. Over the Holy Corridor has survived a mezzanine with "an observation deck", which was used by the women and children of the royal house to watch receptions held in the Throne Room.

View of the Faceted Palace (right), the Annunciation Cathedral and the façade of the Great Kremlin Palace from the Ivan the Great Bell-Tower.
Portals in the Holy Anteroom of the Faceted Chamber.
The Main Throne Room of the Faceted Chamber

The Great Kremlin Palace

Towards the early 19th century the palace complex in the Kremlin included several buildings put up in different periods, but none of them was fully suitable for a stay of the royal court during majestic ceremonies. In the 1830s Nicholas I took a decision to build a new palace to a design by Konstantin Thon and Feodor Solntsev (the latter was responsible for the artistic aspect of the project). There was also a decision that the Faceted Chamber and the Terem Palace should be preserved intact and connected with the new palace by passages. The palace, originally called the Great Nicholas Palace, was under construction for twelve years and a ceremony of its opening was held on 22 August 1851 – in honour of the 25th anniversary of Nicholas I's coronation. Its central block with a belvedere crowned by a flagstaff tower faces the Moskva River, where it affords the most spectacular view of the Kremlin Embankment. The palace interiors include galleries of the state rooms and drawing rooms on the first floor. These interiors strike visitors by their majesty and exquisite luxury. Five rooms in the palace are known as the order halls and they are dedicated to the Russian Orders of St Andrew the First-Called, St Alexander Nevsky, St Prince Vladimir, St George and St Catherine.

View of the Great Kremlin Palace from the Moskva River. The St George Hall

The Enfilade
of Her Majesty's
Own Apartments.
The Large (Green)
Drawing Room
of Her Majesty's
Own Apartments

The Red Drawing
Room (State
Bedchamber)
of Her Majesty's
Own Apartments.
Detail of the interior
of the Large (Green)
Drawing Room

The Great Kremlin Palace 27

The Terem Palace

The Terem Palace, a picturesque building with a high four-slope roof, an observation tower, covered galleries, porches and staircases, was constructed in 1635–36 for Tsar Mikhail Feodorovich by the architects Bazhen Ogurtsov, Antip Konstantinov, Trefil Sharutin and Larion Ushakov. In fact this is a three-storey stone superstructure over the late 15th-century chambers, because the base of the Terem Palace rests on two stone storeys from the age of Ivan III. The enfilade of the royal interiors arranged on the second floor of the palace includes five rooms of nearly equal dimensions covered by coved vaults. These are the Refectory, the Cross and Throne Chambers, the Bedchamber and the Prayer Room. Their interiors are embellished by richly adorned portals and window surrounds, tiled stoves and elaborate painted decorations. The Throne Chamber served as the Tsar's study. The middle window of the room was named the "petition window" – legend has it that a box was descended from it which was accessible for petitioners to the Tsar. The petitions were not considered for years, therefore the box was called the "long-term box" and the expression turned into a set phrase. The Tsar's apartments were connected with the Verknespassky Cathedral by a gallery, and an exit to it was decorated in 1670 by a fine openwork railing with a small gate that became known as "the Golden Railing".

The Terem Palace. View from the inner courtyard of the Great Kremlin Palace. The Cross Chamber of the Terem Palace. The Throne Chamber (Study) of the Terem Palace

The Armoury

The Armoury is one of the world's most famous museums, a treasure-house preserving the unique symbols of Russian statehood. The history of this chamber goes back to the treasury of the Moscow princes, which was kept in the basements of the Annunciation Cathedral. Under Ivan III the treasury was transferred to the specially built Treasure House (architect Marco Ruffo, 1485). The first mention of the "Armoury Chambers" – a workshop attached to the Treasury – dates from 1537. By the end of the 17th century it developed into a set of workshops where armourers, jewellers, enamellers, icon-painters, carvers and other master craftsmen did their work. After the fire of 1737 the Kremlin treasures were transferred to the Terem Palace and in 1809 to a special building of the museum called the Armoury. The building we see now was constructed to a design by Konstantin Thon on the site of the royal stables simultaneously with the Great Kremlin Palace, with which the Armoury is connected by a passage gallery. The collections of the museum number about 4,000 exhibits of exceptional value. Among them are unique works of ancient Russian jewellery, the Tsars' and Emperors' regalia, official costumes, arms and armour, carriages, items of horse attire, diplomatic gifts and the royal thrones. In the two rooms of the lower storey of the Armoury is arranged the "Diamond Fund" exhibition of the Ministry of Finance, where celebrated royal crowns, orders, jewellery, precious stones, gold nuggets, etc., are on display.

View of the Armoury from the Kremlin Embankment.
Exhibits of the Armoury.
Display of Russian gold and silverware of the 12th to early 20th century

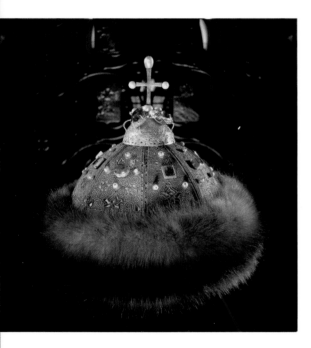

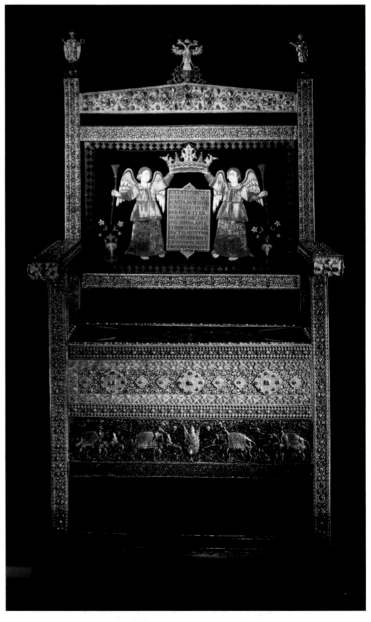

Golden *barmas* from the Ryazan hoard of the 12th–13th century

Silver chalice commissioned by Yuri Vsevolodovich, Prince of Vladimir-Suzdal Principality, grandson of Yuri Dolgoruky, Early 13th century

Monomakh's Cap. Late 13th – early 14th century

The Diamond Throne of Tsar Alexey Mikhailovich. Persia. 1659

The Hall of Russian Arms and Armour

Showcase with Western European armour

Coronation dress
of Empress Catherine II.
1762

Masked ball dress
of Empress Catherine I.
1720s

Showcase with
18th-century costumes

Collection of royal
carriages

The Imperial regalia displayed at the Diamond Fund exhibition

The brilliant badge of the Order of St Andrew the First-Called on a brilliant chain. 1795

Tafelstein diamond (25 carats) with a portrait of Alexander I. Late 1820s

Easter egg: *300th Anniversary of the Romanov House*. Fabergé Company. 1913

Diamond: *Shakh*. (88.7 carats)

In the Historical Centre of Moscow

Like all early capitals of Europe, until the end of the 18th century Moscow was growing along the perimeter of its historical core – the Kremlin and Kitay-Gorod. This caused its famous radial and circular layout. From the Kremlin diverge early radial roads developed into streets, which are crossed by circular thoroughfares laid down on the sites of medieval defensive structures. The earliest section of Moscow lies within the Sadovoye (Garden) Ring, about 5 kilometres in diameter, where it divides into historical districts known as Khamovniki, Arbat, Tverskaya, Lubianka, Sretenka, Ivanovskaya Hill, Kulishki, Zayauzye, Taganka and Zamoskvorechye.

The most ancient part of Moscow outside the Kremlin is Kitay-Gorod – the former great settlement occupying the north-east gentle slope of Borovitsky Hill. In the narrow streets of Kitay-Gorod retaining their layout since the 14th century and meandering between trade rows and other business buildings stand the Romanov boyars' chambers, where, according to a legend, Mikhail Romanov, the founder of the royal dynasty, was born in 1596; the English Courtyard – one of the earliest civic structures of Moscow; the chambers of the Printing Yard and the Synodal Printing House, as well as a number of beautiful churches, examples of the "Moscow style" and the "Naryshkin Baroque". On the side of Teatralny Passage one can see the remains of the Kitay-Gorod fortifications erected in 1535–38 by the architect Petrok Maly and demolished in the Soviet times.

Along the north-western boundary of the Kremlin and Kitai-Gorod, at the foot of Borovitsky Hill, flows a tributary of the Moskva River – the Neglinnaya River, which is nowadays bound in the underground tunnel. The right-hand bank of the Neglinnaya, opposite the Kremlin, was named the Zaneglimenye area. Here, on Vagankovo Hill, where the Pashkov House soars today, Grand Princess Sophia Vitovna set up her palace in the 15th century; she bequeathed the estate to her grandsons. This predetermined the aristocratic character of the Zaneglimenye area, which since then has been built over by palaces of the "nearest" boyars, the Tsar's relations. In the 18th century, when, a complex of Moscow University was built, Zaneglimenye began to acquire the status of Moscow's educational centre, too. In the 1820s the Neglinnaya River was hidden in the underground collector ("pipe") and the former river embankments turned into wide avenues, or *prospekts*, and squares – these are Teatralny Passage with Theatre Square and the majestic Bolshoy Theatre – the main opera and ballet stage of Russia, the Okhotny Ryad with the building of the State Duma, Mokhovaya Street, the already mentioned famous Pashkov House, the old complex of Moscow University and the State Russian Library.

From Zaglimenye radiate fashionable Moscow streets – Volkhonka, Znamenka, Vozdvizhenka, Dmitrovka, Tverskaya, Nikitskaya and Petrovka Streets. This is a reasonably fashionable part of Moscow, which rivals the most expensive urban districts of the world in the luxury of its hotels and shops, in the abundance of its theatres and gorgeous buildings. By the early 20th century the "industry of luxury and fashions" concentrated around Petrovka Street, leading to the Vysoko-Petrovsky Monastery. One of its focal centres also became Kuznetsky Most Street, which crosses Petrovka Street. It owes its name to the bridge that once spanned the Neglinnaya River.

The northern and north-eastern sectors – between the Neglinnaya and Yauza Rivers – had since time immemorial been populated by craftsmen and businessmen, including foreign artisans. One can also find there the celebrated "Moscow's Montmartre" – Tsvetnoy Boulevard with the city's oldest circus, the poetic Chistiye Prudy area, the cosy Kulishki with numerous churches and temples, including a synagogue and a Lutheran church.

Further clockwise are located the Zayauzye area with Taganka Street – originally a trade and industry quarter with settlements of blacksmiths and potters and later a suburb with urban estates and monasteries, which even now represent the main charm of this locality.

At last, to the south of the Kremlin, beyond the Moskva River – in its abrupt bend – spreads the patriarchal Zamoskvorechye area, where the ancestors of the Tretyakov, Riabushinsky, Bakhrushin and other richest merchant families settled in the 18th and 19th centuries. It is in Zamoskvorechye that the Tretyakov Gallery founded by Pavel Tretyakov is situated, as is the Theatrical Museum created by Alexey Bakhrushin. Worthy of mention is also the memorial house of the great playwright Alexander Ostrovsky. The Zamokvorechye area is famous for its numerous churches, too.

One's acquaintance with the highlights of the historical centre of Moscow traditionally begins from Red Square – one of the vastest (2.3 hectares), earliest and most beautiful squares of Europe. An exit from the Kremlin in this direction leads through the gate of the Saviour Tower. At the south-west the square is limited by the Kremlin wall. Near it after the revolution of 1917 was organized a necropolis, the principal structure of which is the Lenin Mausoleum (1930). In the north-east the square is limited by the buildings of the Upper and Middle Trade Rows. At the highest point of the square, near a descent to the Moskva River, stands the world-famous Cathedral of the Intercession-on-the-Moat, which is better known as "Cathedral of St Basil the Blessed".

In the Historical Centre of Moscow

Cathedral of the Intercession-on-the-Moat (Cathedral of St Basil the Blessed)

This cathedral, a superb structure 65 metres high, crowned with a tent-shaped top and eight varicoloured relief domes, strikes one by its impeccable architectonics combined with a wealth of thoroughly worked out jewel-like decoration. It was built by orders of Ivan the Terrible in 1554–63. The addition to the name, "on-the-Moat", reminds us about the Alevis Moat of the early 16th century that was filled in with earth by 1815. The cathedral belongs to the centric type of churches: eight chapels adjoin its central volume like "petals". Originally the chapels were crowned with simple helmet-shaped cupolas. The present onion-shaped, variously coloured domes date from the middle of the 17th century. The main, central chancel of the cathedral is consecrated to the Intercession of the Virgin, the eastern one to the Holy Trinity, in memory of the wooden Church of the Holy Trinity that had stood on the site of the cathedral – it was by the walls of this church that the famous Moscow holy fool Basil was buried. The venerable relics of the saint, "found" in 1588, are kept in the special lower church of the cathedral.

In front of the cathedral stands a monument unveiled in 1818, a work of Ivan Martos, which represents Prince Dmitry Pozharsky and the merchant Kuzma Minin, who raised a volunteer force to fight the invading Poles in 1612. Near the monument stands a round stone pediment – the so-called Lobnoye Mesto. First mentioned in 1547, it served as a tribune from which state decrees and sentences were declared.

**View of the Cathedral of St Basil the Blessed from Red Square.
Tomb of St Basil the Blessed.
Monument to Minin and Pozharsky**

The Upper Trade Rows

Unlike the majority of historical squares, Red Square has a definite date of its creation – 1493. A great fire that raged in Moscow had reached the Kremlin a year before this date. After that Ivan III issued a decree that the territory by the walls of the Kremlin be cleaned from all kinds of structures at a distance of about 250 metres (the length of a cannon shot in that period). Thus a square originally named "Fire" has emerged. To fix its boundaries with Kitay-Gorod stone trade rows were built in the late 16th century. Later they were repeatedly reconstructed and changed their appearance. The architectural complex of the trade rows we can see now dates from the 1890s and was created for Upper Trade Rows Joint-Stock Company to a design by Alexander Pomerantsev. Today it is the largest trade centre of Moscow. The upper trade rows include three galleries with a general area of about 25,000 square metres, covered by glazed steel arched vaults designed by the outstanding engineer Vladimir Shukhov.

To the left of the Upper Trade Rows building stands the graceful Kazan Cathedral, founded in 1630 for the Kazan icon of the Mother of God, which had accompanied Prince Pozharsky during the liberation of Moscow from the Poles in 1612.

The Upper Trade Rows in festive illumination.
The Kazan Cathedral.
Central Hall of the Upper Trade Rows

Manezhnaya (or Manège) Square

On the north-western side Red Square is completed by the building of the State Historical Museum in the "Russian style" put up to a design by Vladimir Sherwood between 1875 and 1881. It occupies the area between the Corner Arsenal Tower and the Resurrection Gate. The gate leads from Red Square to the former Resurrection Square that merged in the 1820s with Manezhnaya or Manège Square. In the 1990s, for the 850th anniversary of Moscow (1997),

In the Historical Centre of Moscow

View of the State Historical Museum and the Corner Arsenal Tower of the Kremlin from Manezhnaya Square

the trade complex Okhotny Ryad was created under Manezhnaya Square. The new trade centre owes its name to the old Moscow market on the bank of the Neglinnaya River. The trade complex was decorated with a cascade fountain and a canal – in memory of the Neglinnaya River bound in the underground pipe. Along the canal are arranged walking terraces. This made the formerly desolate Manezhnaya Square one of the most lively areas in Moscow.

View of the Cathedral of St Basil the Blessed from the garden on Manezhnaya Square ↱

In the Historical Centre of Moscow

Alexander Gardens

The famous gardens near the Kremlin wall – running parallel to Manezhnaya Square – were created to a design by Osip Bove in the 1820s on the site of the Neglinnaya River put into the underground pipe. From the middle of the 19th century the gardens bear the name of Alexander I and a monument to this emperor was set up in 2014. The most celebrated monument in the gardens is "the Tomb of an Unknown Soldier" dedicated to the soldiers killed at the fronts of the Great Patriotic War of 1941–45. The memorial was unveiled in 1967; the Eternal Fire was lit up and an honourary guard, Post No 1, was organized.

The main entrance to the gardens is embellished with a cast-iron Empire-style gate on a railing of spearheads designed by Eugene Pascal. A similar gate was originally erected at the entrance from the Moskva River, but it was dismantled in 1872. The pillars of the gate are crowned by double-headed armorial eagles each holding a thunderbolt in its claws. The wings of the gate are decorated by compositions of crossed arrows and stylized shields with gorgoneions – mask-like representations of Medusa the Gorgon. Over the central avenue of the garden hangs the arch of the Trinity Bridge, one of the earliest bridges that spanned the Neglinnaya River. Near the entrance to this bridge was put up a diverging barbican structure, the Kutafya Tower, which is now part of the Alexander Gardens complex.

The Main Gate of the Alexander Gardens.
Honourary guards near the memorial
"Tomb of an Unknown Soldier".
Monument to Alexander I
in the Alexander Gardens

In the Historical Centre of Moscow

Kitay-Gorod

Church of the Trinity at Nikitniki.
View of Varvarka Street near the Romanov
boyars' chambers.
The building of the English Yard

Kitay-Gorod is one of the earliest districts of Moscow, formed on the site of a trade and handicraft settlement (Veliky Posad) east of the Kremlin. In the 12th century ploughland was still interspersed with forests and rare structures did not promise that several centuries later the eastern slope of Borovitsky Hill would develop into a commercial centre of the Moscow State. Archaeologists have found here, in the layers dating from the 12th and 13th centuries, writings on birch-bark and a large number of locally produced or brought articles. This testifies to the development of handicrafts in medieval Moscow, and also to well-maintained trade ties, which promoted the development of Kitay-Gorod, where soon nearly all Moscow trade would be concentrated. Varvarka Street, preserved as a memorial zone of the early Kitay-Gorod, runs along the edge of Borovitsky Hill from Red Square to Staraya (Old) Square, which is well-known today by its complex of government buildings. On the slope of the hill descending to the Moskva River lies the southern and most ancient section of Kitay-Gorod. Varvarka Street and its surroundings boast a great number of sights, including the medieval chambers of the English Yard, and the courtyard of the Romanov boyars, the Church of the Holy Trinity at Nikitniki built in 1631–34 and decorated with icons of the Tsar's painter Simon Ushakov who lived in Ipatyevsky Lane.

Teatralny Passage and Theatre Square

Teatralny (Theatre) Passage, a short and wide street between Manezhnaya and Lubianka Squares, was created in the 1820s on the site of the original bed of the Neglinnaya River. It is connected with Kitay-Gorod by a short passage in the Kitay-Gorod Wall named the Tretyakov Passage. Built in the late 1860s as a commission of the Tretyakov brothers, Sergey and Pavel, it is decorated with an ornate gate, which makes up a picturesque ensemble with the medieval Bird Half-Tower of Kitay-Gorod. To the left of the gate arch on a granite pedestal stands a monument to the first Russian printer Ivan Fyodorov, an outstanding figure of the age of Ivan the Terrible. The monument created after a model by Sergey Volnukhin, was unveiled in a majestic atmosphere on 27 September 1909 in the presence of a great number of people.

To the right of the Tretyakov Passage gate soars the Metropol, the most famous Moscow hotel built between 1899 and 1904. A whole constellation of eminent Moscow architects and artists, including William Walcott, Lev Kekushev, Ivan Zholtovsky, Mikhail Vrubel, Konstantin Korovin, Vasily Polenov, Alexander Golovin and Sergey Chekhonin took part in its creation. The Metropol Hotel is an integral part of the ensemble of Theatre Square, which was created in 1817–24 on the territory of about 30 hectares by the architect Osip Bove. The principal decoration of the square is the monumental building of the Bolshoy Theatre.

View of the Metropol Hotel from Theatre Square.
Monument to Ivan Fyodorov.
View of the Vitali Fountain, the Round Tower of Kitay-Gorod and the tower of the Saviour Cathedral of the Zaikonospassky Monastery from Theatre Square

The Bolshoy Theatre

The majestic building with a powerful portico, dominating the entire ensemble of Theatre Square, is famous as one of the world' best ballet and opera stages. The theatre was built in the 1820s to a design by the architect Andrey Mikhailov and restored after a fire of 1853 by the architect Albert Cavos. The décor of the fronts was then refurbished and the alabaster composition crowning the portico was replaced by the now famous *Apollo's Chariot*, executed in bronze after a model by the outstanding sculptor Peter Klodt. At the same time the auditorium was built over, the ceiling of which was decorated with the composition *Apollo and the Muses* created by the artist Alexey Titov. The theatre opened on 20 August 1856 – for the festivities on the occasion of Alexander II's coronation. Towards the end of the 19th century it began to rival the Mariinsky Theatre of St Petersburg in the quality of its stage productions. On the stage of the Bolshoy performed Feodor Chaliapin and Leonid Sobinov, Sergey Rakhmaninov conducted the orchestra and stage sets were designed by Apollinary Vasnetsov, Alexander Golovin, and Konstantin Korovin. In the 1920s and 1930s on the stage of the Bolshoy Theatre performed Nadezhda Obukhova, Ivan Kozlovsky and Sergey Lemeshev. The Bolshoy enjoyed a veritable triumph in the post-war years, when, on Stalin's order, to the ballet troupe of the Bolshoy were transferred from Leningrad some great masters of the former Mariinsky Theatre with its powerful academic traditions. Among them were the bewildering Galina Ulanova and the outstanding ballet master Yuri Grigorovich. The stage of the Bolshoy Theatre, on which were shining Maya Plisetskaya, Maris Liepa, Vladimir Vasilyev, Yekateria Vasilyeva, Natalya Bessmertnova and many outstanding dancers became one of the most prestigious in the world. In 1964 this stage saw a triumphal performance of Marlen Dietrich.

View of the Bolshoy Theatre building from a parterre with fountains. The opera *Khovanshchina* by Modest Mussorgsky on the stage of the Bolshoy Theatre

Mokhovaya Street

Before the 19th century Mokhovaya Street had been an embankment of the Neglinnaya River. Today the street is a busy thoroughfare about 850 metres long connecting Manezhnaya and Borovitskaya Squares. The ensemble of Mokhovaya Street is made up of architectural monuments dating from the 18th to 20th century. The most famous among them are the complex of Moscow University with the Church of St Tatyana, the Manège, the Pashkov House and the large-scale building of the Russian State Library (formerly the Lenin Library), in honour of which has been named "The Lenin Library" Metro Station opened on 15 May 1935.

The Manège building is one of the most beautiful Empire-style structures in Moscow. It was put up between 1817 and 1825 to a design by Osip Bove "to commemorate the victory of the Russian people in the Patriotic War of 1812". Auguste de Béthencourt designed for the Manège a unique structure of wooden rafters covering the 45-metre span without additional supports. From 1831 onwards the Manège has served as Moscow's central exhibition hall.

The house of Pyotr Pashkov, completing the ensemble of Mokhovaya Street, stands at the top of Vagankovsky Hill. This beautiful Classicist mansion with a belvedere tower was built in the 1780s to a design by an unknown architect. Today it houses the Manuscript Department of the Russian State Library.

View of the Manège building from Manezhnaya Square.
Dome of the Okhotny Ryad trade centre.
The Pashkov House on Vagankovsky Hill

Panorama of Khamovniki with a view of the Cathedral of Christ the Redeemer ↱

The Pushkin Museum of Fine Arts

Mokhovaya Street beyond Borovitskaya Square continues as Volkhonka Street leading to the ancient Moscow locality known as Chertorye (or Chertolye), a part of the vast Khamovniki area. In the 19th century Volkhonka, as well as Ostozhenka and Prechistenka Streets continuing it, turned into an aristocratic suburb – "St Germain de Moscou", as Prince Piotr Kropotkin, a well-known anarchist, expressed it. On Volkhonka in the middle of the 19th century was set up the grand Cathedral of Christ the Redeemer and opposite it, on the site of the Stable Courtyard that had been founded by Ivan the Terrible, in 1898–1912 was built the Museum of Fine Arts. Today this museum, named the State Pushkin Museum of Fine Arts in the Soviet period, is one of five largest museum of the world. Its building was designed by Roman Klein, who implemented the Art Nouveau concept of a "new temple of art". For this purpose he combined in the museum's architecture a simple and functional volume with an elegant decoration of its fronts in an ancient style. The glazed vaults on metal structures that allowed to achieve an ideal lighting of the interiors, were designed by the prominent engineer Vladimir Shukhov, "a master of economic construction". The rooms and halls of the museum were decorated in various styles reproducing the atmosphere of different ages. The design of the interiors was carried out by the outstanding artists Alexander Golovin and Ignaty Nivinsky, who became also famous as theatrical decorators.

Today the basic displays of the museum are shown in the rooms and halls of the historical building and the famous collection of works by Impressionist and Post-Impressionists is represented in the nearby Gallery of European and American Art of the 19th and 20th centuries.

The main portico of the State Museum of Fine Arts

The Italian Courtyard. Art of Ancient Italy and Ancient Rome

Portrait of a Young Man. Ancient Egypt.
First half of the 2nd century

PIETER PAUL RUBENS (SCHOOL). *The Virgin Presenting the Rosary to St Dominic.* 1630s

REMBRANDT HARMENSZ VAN RIJN. *Ahasuerus, Haman and Ester.* 1660

In the Historical Centre of Moscow

AUGUSTE RENOIR. *Girl in Black*. 1880–82

View of the Cathedral of Christ the Redeemer
from the Moskva River.
Interior of the Cathedral of Christ the Redeemer.
Monument to Emperor Alexander II

Cathedral of Christ the Redeemer

The cathedral occupies a plateau at the top of Chertolye Hill, where once had stood the celebrated Tower with Seven Tops of the White (Tsar) Town – a powerful fortification structure defending the approaches to Moscow near a ford across the Moskva River. At the end of the 18th century the walls and towers of the White Town were demolished and the strengthened area under the Tower with Seven Tops was chosen by Nicholas I for the construction of Russia's most grandiose cathedral. The building of the cathedral lasted for about 40 years (from 1839 to 1883). It is dedicated to the "eternal memory and that unparalleled effort, faithfulness and love for the fatherland, which were demonstrated by the Russian people in the war against Napoleon. The project of the building was created by Konstantin Thon. The scale of the cathedral (103 m high, it could accommodate about 10,000 worshippers) made it the largest structure of Moscow for a long time, while the wealth of its décor (inner facing of labradorite, Shoksha porphyry and Italian marble) was the most luxurious one. Nevertheless in December 1931 the cathedral was blown up. It was recreated in 1996 by the efforts of the Moscow restoration Fund and in the same year the Patriarch consecrated the main cross of the cathedral mounted on the dome in a majestic atmosphere.

Mansion by Lev Kekushev.
House of the engineer Pyotr Pertsov.
Mansion of Alexandra Derozhinskaya. General view
from Kropotkinsky Lane and a staircase in the interior.
Mansion of Stepan Ryabushinsky near the Nikitsky Gate.
Staircase in the interior of Ryabushinsky's mansion.
Mansion of Arseny Morozov on Vozdvizhenka Street
near the Arbat Gate

Moscow Art Nouveau

The Art Nouveau style, which became popular in Moscow in the 1890s, differs from the classical European Art Moderne in that it gave especial preference to historical stylizations. The streets and lanes of the Khamovniki area between Ostozhenka and Prechistenka are famous for mansions in this fashionable genre of the "urban villa" and tenement houses, built by such Art Nouveau masters as Feodor Shekhtel, Lev Kekushev, William Walcott and many others. Illustrious examples are the house of the engineer Pyotr Pertsov "in the Russian style" (1906–07, to sketches by Sergey Malyutin), standing next to the Cathedral of Christ the Redeemer, the castle-mansion of the merchant Vasily Nosov in Ostozhenka Street, a work by Lev Kekushev, and an elegant mansion of Alexandra Derzhinskaya, daughter of a textile tycoon, which is regarded as one of Feodor Shekhtel's creations (1903). Many mansions in the Art Nouveau manner can be found in the picturesque surroundings of Arbat and Tverskaya Streets, which became fashionable among the wealthy Moscow bourgeoisie in the early 20th century. The most famous among them are Arseny Morozov's mansion built in 1894–99 near Arbatskiye Vorota Square and strikingly similar to a Moresque castle, as well as the mansions of the Riabushinskys, nicknamed the "Russian Rothschields", near Nikitskiye Vorota (1900–03) and Savva Morozov's mansion in Spiridonovka Street (1890s).

In the Historical Centre of Moscow

Pedestrian Streets

There is a large number of pedestrian zones in the historical part of the city and their number continues to increase. Pedestrian zones attract numerous tourists as they afford a possibility to abandon the hustle of a noisy megalopolis and inhale an atmosphere of an old city. To the north and north-east of the Kremlin lies the pedestrian Nikoskaya Street of Kitay-Gorod and a vast pedestrian zone including Bolshaya Dmitrovka Street with Kuznetsky Most Street crossing it. Recently the ancient Pokrovka and Maroseika Streets have also been given to pedestrians, as well as the Krymskaya Embankment and the surroundings of the Tretyakov Gallery (Lavrushinsky Lane, Bolshoy Tolmachevsky Lane, Ordynsky Tupik and Klementovsky Lane near the Church of St Clement, the Pope of Rome) in the Zamoskvorechye area. But the main centre of attraction for tourists for three decades now has been Old Arbat – a pedestrian street, more than a kilometre long. It abounds with cafés, restaurants and small museums, including the Memorial Flat of Alexander Pushkin.

View of Arbat Street. Nikolskaya Street in Kitay-Gorod.
View of Kunsnetsky Most Street

In the Historical Centre of Moscow

Tverskaya Street

Monument to Prince Yuri Dolgoruky on Tverskaya Square. Tverskaya Square with a view of the Moscow Government building

Tverskaya Street is the most fashionable street of the capital, one of the most expensive streets in the world rivalling Oxford Street, Ginza, Broadway and the Avenue des Champs-Elysées. Even in the Middle Ages this ancient road from Moscow to Tver was one of Moscow's major thoroughfares. In the 18th century Tverskaya became the beginning of the road leading to the new capital, St Petersburg. The street was used by imperial corteges; palaces of eminent noblemen were built on it, including a residence of the Governor of Moscow (now the Moscow Mayor's Office); it was a street of the best shops and expensive aristocratic clubs. In the Soviet period the street, renamed Gorky Street, became an official thoroughfare of the Soviet capital. In the 1930s the street was widened from 20 to about 50 metres. Some old structures, including all churches, were destroyed and the remaining buildings were moved to the "red line" using the technology invented by the engineer Emmanuil Gendel. The sites of the demolished buildings were replaced by huge dwelling houses with flats of the new Soviet elite – the eminent representatives of culture, scholars, army leaders and officials. In 1954 one of Moscow's symbols – the monument to its founder, Prince Yuri Dolgoruky, was unveiled on Tverskaya Street.

Pushkinskaya Square

Pushkinskaya Square, once named Tverskiye Gate Square (after the Tver Gate of the White Town) and also Strastnaya (Passions) Square (after the Passions Monastery) lies at the crossing of Tverskaya Street with the Boulevard Ring. In the 18th century it was the site where triumphal gates were erected in honour of Russian military victories. In 1938 the square was given the name of Pushkin, a great Russian poet and the founder of the

Pushkinskaya Square with a view of the monument to Alexander Pushkin and the *Rossiya* cinema building

contemporary Russian language, as his monument stood on this square. The monument was created for the funds collected by people in the course of 20 years and was unveiled in a majestic atmosphere on 6 June 1880. It was designed by the sculptor Alexander Anikushin. In 1961 in the depth of the square, behind the monument, was built the Russija Cinema – the largest in Europe in that period (with the auditorium for 2000 seats) and famous as the central building of the Moscow International Film Festivals.

Cathedral of the Immaculate Conception of the Blessed Virgin Mary.
Cathedral of the Nativity of Mother of God at Putniki.
The Menshikov Tower (Church of the Archangel Gabriel).
The Vysoko-Petrovsky Monastery

In the Historical Centre of Moscow

Churches and Monasteries of the White Town

The "radial" streets of Moscow in the Middle Ages had plenty of churches and monasteries, some of which survived to our days. One of them is the ensemble of the Vysoko-Petrovsky Monastery associated with the names of Ivan Kalita, Vasily III and Tsarina Natalia Kirillovna Naryshkina. The Sretensky, Rozhdestvensky and Ivanovsky monasteries, the "lacy" Church of the Nativity of the Virgin at Putinki – the last tent-shaped church in Moscow, the Church of the Archangel Gabriel near Chistiye Prudy (the Menshikov Tower) – a fine example of the Petrine Baroque, created by an outstanding master Ivan Zarudny on the estate of Alexander Menshikov, and any others. A place apart belongs here to non-Orthodox churches: the Moscow synagogue and the Lutheran church on Ivanovskaya Hill, the historical mosque at Zamoskvorechye as well as the Catholic Cathedral of the Immaculate Conception of the Virgin Mary standing behind the Garden Ring, at Presnya, which is the largest Catholic church in Russia.

Historical Shopping Centres

Moscow has been a major commercial centre of the Russian state since the 15th century and therefore not only Russian, but European business-men sought to establish their trade here. This predetermined the creation of numerous trade centres in Moscow. By the beginning of the 20th century the most famous in the city were the Upper Trade Rows (called GUM in the Soviet period) on Red Square, the Gostiny Dvor next to the Stock Exchange in Kitay-Gorod, the Mur and Merilise department store on Theatre Square, the Petrovsky Passage on Petrovka Street, and many others. At the same time were created luxurious specialized shops, which still enjoy great popularity to the present day. These are the Yeliseyev Grocery on Tverskaya Street and the Tea-Coffee Shop on Miasnitskaya with their fascinating interiors. The former was opened by the Brothers Yeliseyev Company from St Petersburg and was widely known for its wine cellars; the second was owned by the tea magnate Sergey Perlov, who had the façade and trade hall of the shop skillfully designed in the Chinese style in 1896.

Tea and coffee shop. General view from Myasnitskaya Street and its interior. The Yeliseyev food shop. Interior and a general view from Tverskaya Street

The Area Beyond the Moskva River

Zamoskvorechye, the area divided from the Kremlin by the Moskva River, is today one of the most picturesque districts of Moscow. Two bridges connect the Kremlin with Zamoskvorechye – the Large Moskvoretsky Bridge and the Large Stone Bridge. To the east of the latter the Moskva River is spanned by the pedestrian Patriarch's Bridge, which affords overwhelming panoramic views of the Moskva River with the Cathedral of Christ the Redeemer and the Kremlin as well as the huge monument to Peter the Great. At the foot of the Patriarch's Bridge one can notice among trees the chambers of the 16th and 17th centuries with a an ornate Church of St Nicholas "behind the Bersenevo railing" – one of the most attractive churches of Zamoskvorechye. The church and palaces rank with the earliest architectural monuments of the crescent-shaped Swamp Island, the name of which reminds us that on the site of the drainage canal once was a swampy shallow branch of the Moskva River. Swamp Island is linked with the "continental" Zamoskvorechye by several bridges, the most well-known among them being the pedestrian Luzhkov Bridge spanning the river between Bolotnaya (Swamp) Square and Lavrushinsky Lane. The later is famous because it leads to the Tretyakov Gallery located on it. The other notable museums of Zamoskvorechye are the Vasily Tropinin Museum devoted to the founder of the Moscow school of realist painting, the Bakhrushin Theatrical Museum housing the world's largest collection on the history of theatrical art, the memorial House of the playwright Ostrovsky, the Russian Museum of Forest representing the history of wooden construction in Moscow. The highlights of the Zamoskvorechye area are also low-rise complexes of Bolshaya Polianka, Piatnitskaya and Bolshaya Ordynka Streets, cosy lanes with graceful mansions and strikingly beautiful churches.

View of the Large Moskvoretsky Bridge and the Rauschskaya Embankment of Zamoskvorechye Moskva River. Church of St Nicholas at Bersenevo. View of the Patriarch's Bridge and the monument to Peter the Great

The State Tretyakov Gallery

This gallery, the collections of which number more than 100,000 works of art, is the world's largest museum of Russian art. The museum's history began in the middle of the 19th century when Pavel Tretyakov, a representative of a rich Moscow family of textile tycoons, who had settled in Moscow a century before, began to collect paintings in his mansion at Zamoskvorechye. The private collection was quickly growing and Tretyakov set a task for himself "to initiate the creation of a public repository of fine arts accessible to everybody." In 1872–74 a special gallery was attached to his mansion and by 1881 it was enlarged. At the same time the gallery was opened for visitors and soon became a favourite place for thousands of well-educated Muscovites. In 1892, six years before his demise, Tretyakov took a decision to bequeath his gallery to the city of Moscow. By 1901 the Tretyakov House was reconstructed and its fronts were decorated in the Russian style from sketches by Victor Vasnetsov. In 1918 the gallery became the property of the state and turned into one of the most valuable objects of its cultural heritage. The complex of the museums includes the 17th-century Church of St Nicholas-at-Tolmachi, once attended by Pavel Tretyakov himself. Today the church has a display of icons from the collections of the Tretyakov Gallery. the most famous of which is the Vladimir Icon of the Mother of God of, a masterpiece of 12th-century Byzantine painting, one of the most sacred icons of the Russian Orthodoxy.

View of the main façade of the Tretyakov Gallery and the monument to Pavel Tretyakov from Lavrushinsky Lane.
The Room of Early Russian Icon-Painting.
Rooms and halls of the Tretyakov Gallery

ANDREY RUBLEV. *The Trinity.* 1420s

In the Historical Centre of Moscow

KARL BRIULLOV. *The Rider.* 1832

MIKHAIL VRUBEL. *The Swan Tsarevna.* 1900

VICTOR VASNETSOV. *The Knights.* 1898

Churches Beyond the Moskva River

There are about fifty functioning churches on the territory of Zamoskvorechye (literally "beyond the Moskva River"), which is 432 hectares in area. Such density of churches is characteristic of Moscow, where by 1917 had been more than 1620 Orthodox altars (they are described in legends as "forty by forty"). The churches in this area are striking for their variety and picturesque quality. These are the austere Church of the Beheading of St John the Baptist-by-the-Forest built by Alevis Novy, the Baroque Church of St Clement, a fine monument of the Art Nouveau style – the complex of the SS Martha and Mary Convent, and a masterpiece of the "Moscow style" – the Church of St Gregory of Neocesarea-at-Derbitsy, decorated by nine thousands of tiles. The latter is remarkable as the church where Tsar Alexey Mikhailovich married Natalia Naryshkina in 1671 and in 1672 his son Piotr, the future Emperor Peter the Great, was baptized.

The Intercession Cathedral of the SS Martha
and Mary Convent.
Church of St Clement, the Roman Pope, at Ordyntsy.
Church of St George of Neocesarea-at-Debritsy.
Church of St George of Neocesarea-at-Debritsy with
a view of the iconostasis

Beyond the Garden Ring

The Garden Ring is a circular road of Moscow about 5 kilometres in diameter and about fifteen kilometres long, which begins its history from the fourth line of Moscow fortifications, known as the Earth Town. These fortifications were created in 1591–92 in a great hurry and had the shape of a rampart and moats filled with water. At the rampart were erected watch and passage towers connected by wooden walls around five metres high. The fortifications were burnt down in the Time of Troubles (1600s), but in 1738 they were completely demolished. After the fire of 1812 the ramparts were razed to the ground and the moats were filled with earth; the ring of empty areas was used to lay out gardens. This led to the creation of the Garden Ring.

The boundaries of Moscow stepped over the borders of the Garden Ring towards the beginning of the 18th century and in the 20th century, when the city's territory grew more than ten times larger, the once distant suburbs with monasteries and estates became a part of Moscow.

Distances between these architectural monuments are quite large and most of them belong to the golden fund of Moscow architecture. These landmarks include churches of the 15th and 16th centuries in grand ducal and royal villages of Kolomenskoye and Dyakovo, the fortified complexes of the Danilov, Novospassky, Simonov, Spaso-Andronikov, Donskoy Monasteries and the Novodevichy Convent (New Convent of the Virgin), as well as the palace and park complexes of the 17th to 19th century. The Danilov and Novospassky Monasteries were founded in the 13th century by Prince Daniil of Moscow – the forefather of Moscow's grand princes and Tsars from the Rurik Dynasty – and became a part of the line of fortified monasteries at the approaches to Moscow from the south and south-east. The Simonov (Assumption) Monastery, also a part of this defensive system, was founded in 1370; in the late 16th century its fortifications were rebuilt in stone under the guidance of the outstanding fortification Feodor Kon. The Andronikov Monastery, located on the high bank of the Yauza River, was a votive monastery of the Moscow Metropolitan St Alexius. The Donskoy Monastery and the New Convent of the Virgin rank with the most picturesque architectural ensembles of the 17th century. From the same century dates the red-brick complex of the Krutitskoye Podvorye. One of the most magnificent churches of the 17th century is the Church of the Intercession at Fili – an example of the Naryshkin Baroque, created on the estate of Lev Naryshkin, Peter the Great's uncle. The estate of Izmaylovo that belonged to Tsar Alexey

Mikhailovich, has been also associated with Peter the Great. The future great emperor spent here his childhood youth and it was on the Izmaylovo ponds that he took his first lessons of navigation, using the English boat St Nicholas, bought for the estate at the beginning of the 17th century.

Between the 18th and 20th centuries in the environs of Moscow were created marvellous summer estates designed in keeping with fashionable European styles – Lefortovo, the Peter Palace, Kuskovo, Tsaritsyno, Perovo, Ostankino, Kuzminki, etc. Ostankino that belonged to the Count Sheremetev family was famous for its palace theatre, while Arkhangelskoye, the estate of the Prince Yusupov family, boasted a fine collection of works of art; Perovo, the estate of the Prince Golitsyn family, was remarkable for the miniature Church of Our Lady of the Sign created by the Swedish architect Nicodemus Tessin the Younger. Legend has it that around 1746 this church was the venue of the secret marriage between Empress Elizabeth Petrovna and Alexey Razumovsky (he became the owner of Perovo in 1744). This church is a replica of the Church of Our Lady of the Sign put up between 1690 and 1704 by Italian architects in the Golitsyns' other estate, Dubrovitsy.

In the Soviet period picturesque forests between the old estates, monasteries and royal villages were partly turned into parks of culture and rest and partly built over with huge complexes of dwellings, sports facilities, memorial, educational and exhibition buildings. Worthy of mention among them are the All-Soviet Exhibition of the Achievements of People's Economy at Ostankino, one of the largest exhibition centres in the world, and an architectural complex at Vorobyovy Gory (Sparrow Hills) on the steep right-hand bank of the Moskva River. The highlight of the latter is the new building of Moscow University. Its central 36-storey block, 240 metres high, crowned with a 58-m spire, stands at the highest point of Moscow – 75 metres above the river level. This is one of the seven "Stalin high-rise buildings", which were erected in the 1940s–1950s and laid a beginning for the "high-rise Moscow", which was further enlarged in the 1960s–1970s by New Arbat Street and the building for the higher bodies of the Russian Federation with the 27-storeyed main block crowned by a clock tower – since 1994 the Government of the Russian Federation building, commonly known as the "White House". In the early 21st century Moscow has been embellished with the "Moscow-City" architectural complex that incorporated more than 30 buildings concentrated on an area of about 100 hectares at the Presnenskaya Embankment of the Moskva River.

High-Rise Buildings

The famous Moscow high-rise buildings, with their silhouettes having something in common with the tent-shaped towers of the Moscow Kremlin, rank among the most remarkable highlights of the Russian capital. The idea of constructing them as a grandiose unified architectural ensemble was suggested by Joseph Stalin in the 1930s, but its full-scale realization began in 1947, to mark the 800th Anniversary of Moscow. Eight high-rise buildings were conceived and seven of them were fully constructed. These are administrative, hotel and dwelling complexes with lavish outside and interior decoration with a wide use of Soviet symbols.

Ukraine Hotel. Ministry of Foreign Affairs building

Moscow University building. Dwelling house on the Kotelnicheskaya Embankment

The Moscow Metro

The Moscow Metro is one of the largest in the world (it has 180 stations with an overall length of the lines of more than 300 kilometres). 44 stations are regarded as objects of cultural heritage.

The construction of the metro began after the government decree adopted in 1931. It was as early as 1935 that the first line, Park Kultury – Sokolniki, consisting of 13 stations, was opened. During their creation engineers, architects and artists succeeded in brilliantly solving functional, spatial and artistic tasks and demonstrated the young Soviet country's striving forward, which made the Moscow Metro the best and most beautiful in the world for that period. This success was confirmed at the World Exhibitions in Brussels (1935) and Paris (1937), where many architectural and engineering solutions of the stations won the Grand-Prix. In the early 1950s, after the grandiose victory of the Soviet Union over Nazi Germany, the Metro became a means of propaganda of the might of the Soviet state. The underground vestibules turned into luxuriously decorated state rooms abundant in sculpture, mosaics and bronze decorations.

Underground halls of the Moscow Metro stations: Novoslobodskaya, Ploshchad Revolyutsii, Park Pobedy, Komsomolskaya-Koltsevaya and Mayakovskaya.

The All-Russian Economic Achievements Centre

The All-Russian Economic Achievements Centre is one of the largest exhibition centres in the world (its territory is about 240 hectares and it has more than 70 pavilions). It was opened on 1 August 1939 near the Ostankino estate as an agricultural exhibition. The architectural complex of the exhibition included monumental pedestals with sculptural groups glorifying the working people: *The Worker and the Kolkhoz Woman* by Vera Mukhina (24 m high) and *The Tractor Driver and the Kolkhoz Woman* (13 m high). The exhibition enjoyed a great success and it was resumed in 1954 and soon got an even wider status and the title of the Exhibition of the Achievements of People's Economy. The central avenue of the exhibition was embellished with fountains: The *Friendship of Peoples* having 800 water jets (1954), The *Stone Flower*, and The *Ear of Wheat*. Next to the exhibition in 1963–67 was built the Ostankino TV Tower (540 m high), a unique free-standing structure with the depth of its foundation just 4.6 metres. In 1964 in a garden near the Exhibition of the Achievements of the People's Economy was unveiled the titanium-clad monument *To the Conquerors of Space* in the form of the starting-up rocket.

Panorama of the All-Russian Exhibition Centre with a view of the main arch, the Central Pavilion and the dome of the Space Pavilion. The USSR Peoples' Friendship fountain on the central avenue at the All-Russian Exhibition Centre. Display in the Space Pavilion

Beyond the Garden Ring

Monuments: *The Worker and the Kolkhoz Woman* and *To the Conquerors of Space*. Ostankino TV Tower

Monuments of Martial Glory

The military history of Moscow consists of hundreds of victories and losses, examples of brave feats and self-sacrifices. The capital of Russia remembers the onslaught of Khan Batu in 1238–39, raids of the Golden Horde khans, the Polish occupation during the Time of Troubles, Napoleon's invasion in 1812 and, eventually, the battle for Moscow (30 September 1941 – 20 April 1942). These events are commemorated in dozens of Moscow monuments, especially notable among which are the memorial complexes on Poklonnaya Hill and at Fili on Kutuzovsky Prospekt – an ancient road leading to Smolensk. There is a whole series of well-known memorials here, within some 1.5 kilometres from Victory Square. These include the panoramic museum "The Battle of Borodino", opened in 1962 – on the eve of the 150th anniversary of the battle. Next to it in 1973 was opened the monument to Mikhail Kutuzov, a work by the sculptor Nikolai Tomsky. On Victory Square stands the Triumphal Gate put up in the 1960s to a design by Osip Bove. To the south of Kutuzovsky Prospekt, on Poklonnaya Hill, on 9 May 1995 was opened the Victory Park dedicated to the warriors killed during, the battle of the Great Patriotic War of 1941–45. The ensemble of the park includes a huge obelisk, *The Victory Monument*, and memorial churches and temples of various confessions.

Panoramic view of the Victory Park complex. In the foreground, the Triumphal Arch on Kutuzovsky Prospekt.
At the foot of the Victory Monument obelisk in the Victory Park.
Monument to Field Marshal Mikhail Kutuzov near the building of the Battle of Borodino Panoramic Museum

Gardens and Parks

More than a hundred gardens and parks are situated on the territory of Moscow. These include historical and scientific-educational ones (such as the celebrated Moscow Zoo, the All-Union Exhibition of Economic Achievements or botanical gardens at Ostankino or near Moscow University), memorial ones (the Victory Park and Fili), sports parks (Luzhniki) and amusements parklands (the Sokolniki Park, the Central Park of Culture and Rest).

The Moscow Zoo, the earliest and largest zoo in Russia, was established in 1864 in the Presnya area upon the initiative of the Imperial Society for the Acclimatization of Animals and Plants. In the Soviet period its territory was markedly enlarged and today it makes up 22 hectares. The Zoo has invariably enjoyed a great success. Even during World War II, from 1941 to 1945, more than six million people visited it. All animals in the zoo are kept in open-air cages and pavilions, where their conditions made as close to natural ones as possible.

Main entrance to the Moscow Zoo.
Polar bears in the open-air pavilion of the Moscow Zoo.
Ponds in the Izmailovsky Park

Among historical parks of Moscow are both small, intimate ones, such as the Aquarium Garden, just a hectare in area, and immense recreation complexes, like Izmaylovo Park, which occupies an area of more than 1600 hectares. The core of Izmaylovo is a unique 17th-century estate ensemble, created by Tsar Alexey Mikhailovich in the valley of the Serebryanka River. Around the estate along the banks of the Serebryanka and sixteen artificial ponds spreads the park of rest and amusements, In 1998–2007 the vast cultural and amusement centre "The Kremlin at Izmaylovo" was created – a fairy-tale stylization of ancient Russian towns with walls and defensive towers, the Church of St Nicholas, chambers housing handicraft centre and small museums.

A special place is occupied in Moscow by numerous estates of the 18th and 19th centuries, the most famous of which are the palace and park ensembles at Tsaritsyno, Kuskovo and Ostankino. Kuskovo, the summer residence of the Count Sheremetev family is famous by its unique collection of porcelain. The Tsaritsyno ensemble created between 1776 and 1785 by Vasily Bazhenov for Empress Catherine the Great strikes its visitors by beautiful buildings in the Gothic style.

View of the Izmailovsky Kremlin complex.
The Kuskovo estate. The Count Sheremetevs Palace.
The Great Palace of the Tsaritsyno Estate

Churches and Monasteries

There are about 900 churches and 30 monasteries and convents in Moscow and in its environs, some of which rank with monuments of the UNESCO world cultural heritage. One of the most beautiful and famous monastery ensembles within the boundaries of the city is the Novodevichy Convent (of the Most Pure Icon of the Smolenskaya Mother

Novodevichy Convent

of God) at Khamovniki, to which Prechistenka Street leads from the Kremlin. The convent was founded by Vasily III in 1523 to mark the end of the war against Poland for the possession of ancient Smolensk, successful for Moscow. In 1524–25 the convent's main cathedral was built and in the late 15th century the walls and towers of the convent were put up, which were decorated in the late 17th century by graceful openwork "crowns".

Churches and Monasteries

The St Andronik Monastery of Our Saviour, standing on the high bank of the Yauza River, was founded in the 14th century by Metropolitan Alexius, the confessor of Dmitry Donskoy. It is one of the earliest in Moscow. This monastery was famous for its rich library and by its own school of copying and illustrating books. In this monastery spent the last years of their lives the monks Andrey Rublev (d. 1430) and his colleague Daniil Cherny, who are buried in the chancel of the Cathedral of Our Saviour.

The Donskoy Monastery, one of the guarding monasteries in the south of Moscow, was founded by Tsar Feodor Ioannovich in memory of the expulsion of the Crimean khan Kazy-Girey from the walls of Moscow. In the late 17th century, during the rule of Peter the Great, his sister Catherine founded here the new (Large) Donskoy Cathedral, in which miraculously survived the 8-tiered iconostasis with icons of "foreign" painting. The basement of the cathedral with the altar of the Meeting of the Lord is the burial vault of the Imeretian Tsar Archil II. In 1686–1711, using the money donated by Yakov Kirillov, son of the Duma deacon Averky Kirillov, the red-brick walls with twelve ornate towers were erected.

The St Andronic Monastery of Our Saviour (right, the Cathedral of the Saviour).
The Great Cathedral of the Icon of Our Lady of the Don in the Donskoy Monastery.
Interior of the Great Cathedral of the Icon of Our Lady of the Don in the Donskoy Monastery with a view of the iconostasis with late 17th-century examples of "foreign-manner" icon-painting

Beyond the Garden Ring

The Krutitskoye Patriarch's Yard is one of the most beautiful architectural ensembles of the late 17th century. The yard was founded in the late 13th century, under Prince Daniil of Moscow, on the steep bank of the Moskva River, on the site known as Krutitsy. Originally that was the monastery of the Saraisk Bishopric established in 1261 in the capital of the Golden Horde. The bishopric played an important role in the diplomatic contacts of the Russian Church and enjoyed a colossal influence.

Kolomenskoye is a grand-ducal (later Tsar's) village on the bank of the Moskva River, the first mention of which dates from 1336. The flowering of Kolomenskoye coincided with the 16th century when a new royal palace was put up here, with the majestic tent-shaped Church of the Ascension of the Lord (1532), created by the Italian architect Petrok Maly Friazin. This unique church until the end of the 16th century was the highest structure in the Russian state (60 metres). Next to the Church of the Ascension in 1649, after the establishment of the general church veneration of the Kazan Icon of the Mother of God was laid down the Kazan Church connected by a gallery with the Palace of Tsar Alexey Mikhailovich.

Southern view of the bell-tower and the Assumption Cathedral of the Krutitsky Patriarch's Yard.
The main ensemble of Kolomenskoye with the Church of the Ascension the Lord (left).
The Kazan icon of the Mother of God from the Kazan Church at Kolomenskoye. 17th century

Bridges across the Moskva River

The Moskva River, a tributary of the Oka, is the main water artery of Moscow, within the boundary of which flows about one sixth of its overall length (80 of 500 kilometres). The level of the river is traditionally counted from the "Moscow zero" – a water mark near the Danilov Monastery. Not very deep (4 to 6 metres) and not very wide (up to 200 metres), the Moskva River usually became quite shallow in summer, so that in the Middle Ages people used to wade it in warm seasons, while in winter they crossed it over ice. The first permanent bridge across the river, the stone All-Saints Bridge that connected the environs of the Kremlin with the area beyond the Moskva River, was built only in the 17th century, in 1643–93.

The flowering of bridge-building in Moscow took place in the 20th century when the majority of Moscow bridges were constructed. Outstanding examples of bridge-building, however, continue to appear even in our days, too. One of these is, for instance, the suspended Zhivopisny (Picturesque) Bridge in the Silver Forest, opened in 2007. On the arch of its pylon, at the height of about 100 metres, was constructed an observation deck. In all, it is possible to cross the Moskva River within Moscow using about forty bridges, including four walking or pedestrian bridges. Among the latter are the Bagration Bridge in the Moscow City complex, the steel arched Bogdan Khmelnitsky Bridge, the similarly designed Pushkin Bridge between the Neskuchy Garden Embankment and the Frunzenskaya Embankment connecting the Berezhkovskaya and Rostovskaya Embankments near the Kiev Station and the Patriarch's Bridge in the ensemble of the Cathedral of Christ the Redeemer.

The Bagration Bridge.
The Zhivopisny
(Picturesque) Bridge.
The Patriarch's Bridge.
The Bogdan Khmel-
nitsky Bridge

↱
Panorama of the
Moskva River with
a view of the Boro-
dinsky and Novoar-
batsky Bridges. In the
background, in the
centre, the building
of the Government
of the Russian federation
("White House")

New Moscow

Although Moscow is a very old city, nowadays it is an immense field for architectural experiments. If in the 1990s the city could be called "a capital of new eclecticism", today architects are increasingly bold in overcoming the continuity of styles and in attempts to create the image of 21st-century Moscow. The first break-through became the high-rise "Moscow City" complex, the creation of which started in the late 1990s. This is an international business centre occupying an area of about 100 hectares on the bank of the Moskva River (the Presnenskaya Embankment). Being one of the most magnificent high-rise ensembles in the world, this complex includes around 30 buildings. These include the "Federation" tower made up of two blocks, the eastern one being the tallest skyscraper in Europe (373 metres). Besides the high-rise complexes, architects are designing in Moscow interesting objects of low height, small-scale architectural forms. Among the most remarkable highlights are the park at Zariadye (the Diller Scofidio + Renfro design studio), a dwelling complex on Ostozhenka Sreet, the Vivaldi Plaza office and hotel centre (Sergey Karasev's Studio), the Praktika Theatre on the Patriarch's Ponds, the Documentary Cinema Centre in the Museum of Moscow (the Wowhaus Bureau) and others.

"Moscow City". The West Tower of the "Federation" complex. The "Red Hills" complex on Bolotny Island beyond the Moskva River. To the right, the Moscow International House of Music. Panoramic view of Kutuzovsky Prospekt with a view of the Moscow City complex

Moscow Baroque

Moscow Baroque of the late 17th century is a style that owes its flowering in Moscow to such important political event as the reunion of western Russian lands with Russia in 1654–67. Thanks to favourable disposition of Tsar Alexey Mikhailovich and the patronage of relations of Tsarina Natalia Kirillovna, many European masters of art began to arrive in Moscow. European influences are especially visible in icon-painting ("foreign" or "lifelike" manner of painting) and in church architecture which, as Yevgeny Trubetskoy later wrote, symbolized in the Russian state "the principle that must dominate in the world". The new style demonstrated Russia's striving to enter a new way of development, discarding the medieval approach to reality. Masterpieces of this style are the churches at Dubrovitsy, the estate of Boris Golitsyn, who was a tutor of Peter the Great, and the church at Phili, the estate of Lev Naryshkin, Peter's uncle.

Church of Our Lady of the Sign (Icon of the Mother of God of the Sign) at Dubrovitsy.
Interior of the Church of Our Lady of the Sign at Dubrovitsy with a view of space under the dome.
Church of the Intercession of the Virgin at Fili

The Trinity-St Sergius Monastery (Laura)

The environs of Moscow – Volokolamvsk, Zvenigorod, Dmitrov, Zaraisk, Kolomna, Serpukhov – are famous thanks to their medieval architectural monuments as well as the ensemble of the Trinity-St Sergius Monastery in Sergiyev Posad. This major Orthodox monastery of Russia (given the status of *laura* or major monastery in 1742), the Archimandrite of which is the Patriarch of Moscow and all Russia, was founded in the 1330s by St Sergius of Radoneszres) are concentrated more than 50 buildings and structures – from monuments of the Early Moscow style to masterpieces of the Elizabethan Baroque. The principal church of the monastery – the Trinity Cathedral – was erected in 1422–23 with money donated by Prince Yuri Zvenigorodsky and became the sepulchre of St Sergius of Radonezh. The cathedral is famous for its iconostasis, in which survive about 40 icons by the great Andrey Rublev, Daniil Cherny and artists of their circle executed in the early 1420s. For this iconostasis Andrey Rublev also painted his world-famous *Trinity*. The monastery walls and towers were erected in the 1540s and 1550s. During the Time of Troubles they withstood a 16-month siege of troops led by Sapiega and Lisowski.

The Assumption Cathedral of the Trinity-St Sergius Monastery.
The Trinity Cathedral of the Trinity-St Sergius Monastery.
The Cathedral of the Holy Trinity. The sepulchre
of St Sergius of Radonezh

General view of the Trinity-St Sergius Monastery ensemble ↱

MOSCOW

Art book

TEXT BY

TATYANA LOBANOVA

DESIGN AND MAKE-UP BY

ALEXANDER LOBANOV

MAP BY THE ARTIST

ALEXANDER SMIRNOV

TRANSLATED FROM THE RUSSIAN BY

VALERY FATEYEV

TECHNICAL PREPARATION BY

A. ILLARIONOV AND A. LOBANOV

PHOTOGRAPHY:

**YU. BATURINA, B. BOCHKAREV, A. GAVRILIN, R. GALEYEV,
I. KHIMIN, I. LITVIAK, A. LOBANOV, A. MARKUSHEV,
K. ORESHKIN, A. PETROV, N. RAKHMANOV, V. SAVIK,
G. SHPIKALOV, AIRPANO, LORI PHOTO BANK**

GOLDEN LION PUBLISHING HOUSE

3 Mira Street, St Petersburg, Russian Federation, 197101

Tel./Fax: (812) 493-5207